SPEAK LIFE

Re-Introducing a Language of Love and Gratitude

Mike Hilson and Robert Watson

ACKNOWLEDGMENTS

This book is dedicated to all those whose stories have intersected ours in such powerful ways. Your words of love, encouragement, affirmation, and trust are told here and have been of utmost importance in our development. It is our prayer that these stories will also help in the development of others. God bless you as He has blessed us through you!

CONTENTS

FORWARD

In the year 2000, Robert Watson and I (Mike Hilson) began having breakfast together once a week. During those hours, we would encourage one another, scold one another, laugh together, pray together, and sometimes cry together. But we always told stories. Family stories, work stories; friend stories, life stories—we always told stories. We are, at our core, storytellers. And God has provided plenty of stories for each of us to tell!

At some point, we decided that we should write these stories down. And so began the book you are now holding. These stories have altered each of our lives. The people who inspire each of them have somehow changed our perspective, our self-image, even our self-worth. And we wanted to somehow share those stories with others. Hopefully, through telling and retelling of these stories, other lives will be altered for the good. Others perspectives, self-images, and even self-worth will be improved and redirected.

As you read, know that we are praying for your story. And we are believing that your story is nowhere near as great as it can be, and nowhere near over. Your best days are ahead, and we hope, in some small way, to speak life into those days.

A MESSAGE FROM ROBERT WATSON

I grew up around a family that loved to tell stories, and, for the most part, they were true. I can remember my grandfather, my mother, my uncles, and even my brothers and sister regaling us all with tales from our family past. I always loved listening to them and even began to share these famous stories with others.

I never would have guessed that those storytelling days of my childhood past would come to be so handy later in life. As an adult, my vocation just happened to lend itself to giving speeches and presentations all over the world, and so I made use of the stories I so loved to hear. After almost every presentation, people would approach me and say, "Robert, you really should write a book." While this statement was flattering, I never quite saw myself writing a book. It seemed to me that a writer had to be highly disciplined and have fairly good writing skills. Neither is a gift I possess. Even so, I occasionally entertained the possibility of one day writing about these tales from the past and my experiences along the way.

When I thought about writing this book, I wondered what I would actually write about. You see, I have cerebral palsy (CP), and I've often been asked to write about what it was like to grow up with CP. However, I've always veered away from the urge to write a niche book. Not that writing about CP and the struggles therein is not significant, but I really wanted to write a book with a positive message that could reach a broader audience. Even then, I could only think of about fifteen people who would buy my book, and three of those fifteen who might actually read it.

Then it dawned on me to write about the individuals who had changed the lives of others—people who were influential through a simple action or statement. My close friend Mike Hilson agreed to coauthor this book with me. He, too, is a storyteller, both in his personal life and in his career. Together, we formed a series of true, life-giving stories that we believe can help readers uncover the pivotal moments in their lives and those who help to influence such moments.

We want people to benefit from realizing, understanding, and sharing their life-speaking moments with others. We also want people to recognize the life speakers throughout their journeys and personally acknowledge those who, perhaps unknowingly, changed their lives for the better. This can be liberating, both for the person saying thanks and the person being recognized. Mike and I should know; we've both done it.

This is a book about positive change—sort of a movement, if you will. There are no opportunities to blame others for my problems, and there is no room for a victim mentality here. The focus is on gratitude for those who have taught us so much, and also for having a teachable spirit that allows crucial people to play pivotal roles in our lives. So why don't you come and join the movement?

INTRODUCTION

Speak Life—a Definition

Although we may not realize it, we all have people who affect our lives and outlook in ways that change us. We are defining these influential people as *life speakers*. Life-speaking people can take everyday mundane situations and somehow turn them into pivotal moments in our development. They give us new insight. They teach us about ourselves and the world around us. They help us to see things differently and, perhaps, better.

Changing one's perspective is not a small thing. Once perspective has changed, then direction can change. Again, a new way of seeing yourself is not a final point of being. It is not arriving at whom you were always meant to be. Remember, this is not a Hollywood movie where people arrive to the sound of a wonderful orchestra at the pinnacle of their lives, with a grand smile and obvious joy, and then slowly fade away into fond memories. Life is generally not like that. Those grand moments do come, but they're followed by other moments. When the proverbial music fades from our moment of beaming glory, life goes on...in good ways, and in bad.

Great moments of insight are followed by moments of great confusion.

Great moments of victory are followed by moments of great failure. Life goes on.

When we've been given a new, healthy perspective on ourselves and our lives, we can take those moments, good and bad, and use them to build a future. They provide our starting point for becoming.

Life is all about becoming. We're always becoming something. In high school, we're becoming adults. In college, we're becoming graduates. In our careers, we're becoming successful. In our family lives, we're becoming spouses...then parents...then grandparents. We are always becoming. Life speakers help us to become. In reality, by shifting our perspective of ourselves and the world around us, they help to shape the people we become. As our lives positively pivot with their advice and/or influence, we find invaluable direction in our journey.

Life speakers arrive just at the right time, when we're ready for a new direction or new perspective. Pivotal moments come when we have run the course of where we are and we are ready for something new. Timing is everything when it comes to life-changing experiences.

You see—at the right moment, in the right setting, with the right heart, from the right person—simple words make profound changes in the way we view ourselves and our future. The words themselves often are not profound, but they result in a profound change in perspective. The change may not be immediately apparent, and the power of a certain phrase or piece of advice may not be realized right away. In fact, of all the accounts listed here, very few resulted in an instant realization of the power of the advice. It can take weeks or months—even years—before the profound nature of a phrase is realized. But, even years later, simple words spoken from a loving heart can bring profound change.

That is the art of speaking life.

Parents, grandparents, brothers, sisters, aunts, uncles, and cousins can speak life. Sometimes, though, life speakers will not be those who are close to you. Teachers, pastors, bosses, friends, and even enemies can bring you to pivotal points in your life. They cause you to take important and monumental turns. They help you to see things differently; they help you to discover new things about yourself. People who speak life change everything. So, let's take a look at a few life speakers from our lives to help you identify a few from yours.

1

SPEAK VALUE

"Mike, sing this."
—*Mrs. Frances Cowan, Mike's high-school chorus teacher*

Realization of ability is the portal for achievement.

It was just another day in hell. At least that's how I viewed high school. Up to this point, high school was no different than middle school, and that was not good news. With no friends, no distinguishing abilities, and no goals, my educational experience was not going well. In fact, it had been a nightmare. While my grades were fine, my life was not. Most mornings were spent completely alone in crowded hallways. No one spoke to me unless they felt the need for that little personal pick-me-up that comes from ridiculing the school nerd who has no friends. Even then, the verbiage directed my way didn't last long. I really hated school.

Upon entering high school, I had to choose my elective classes. I really didn't have much of an opinion, so I chose chorus. When I was a kid, I had done some singing in the children's choir at the church my family attended. They had even allowed me to sing a couple of solos. Unfortunately, the leadership at that church had decided my family didn't belong there and had ostracized us all from the congregation. In the process, I lost all my friends and started the lonely, downward spiral that had led to this moment. Nevertheless, I had fond memories of singing in the choir...so I had signed up for chorus, which brings us back to that day—just another day in hell.

It was early in the school day and fairly early in the school year. I was seated in the back row of the choir with my voice section, and we were practicing a song we may or may not have been preparing to perform later. To be honest, I don't even remember what song we were singing, but I remember that I was familiar enough with it that I knew the words and the tune. And that's when she said it. Mrs. Frances Cowan, the chorus teacher, looked up at me and said three words that I can still hear ringing in my ears: "Mike, sing this."

I was stunned. I had rarely even been spoken to, much less been the center of attention. I had not sung in front of anyone for probably four years. My heart started racing, and my mind was a blur. Mrs. Cowan just started playing the song. I thought to myself, "The words! What are the words?" My mind raced until I remembered the first few words to the song. Once I had those in mind, I was certain I could sing the entire song if necessary. And then I sang it...and everything changed.

I will never forget that moment. There were probably thirty to forty kids in that choir, and as I started to sing, their heads began to turn. I watched as a few of their mouths went slightly ajar. Their eyes seemed to question what was happening, and if they could have said something at that moment, I imagined they would have said, "Where did that come from?" Mostly they just stared and listened. Perhaps for the first time since elementary school, people were actually listening to me. They were not yelling at me. They were not picking on me. They were not insulting me. They were listening. When the verse was over, the room exploded in applause, and everything changed for me—at that moment.

From that moment on, high school was no longer hell. That day I became known for something. I began to make friends and work toward some goals in my high-school life. I began to attend conferences and camps for music, and ultimately, I entered college to study music education. Though that would not be my final career choice, music had changed my life forever. Actually, let's be more precise here: Mrs. Frances Cowan had changed my life forever. She had heard something preceding rehearsal that brought her to that pivotal place in my life. She paid attention to a kid that no one else paid attention to and found in him—in me—a talent that no one else, including myself, knew I even had. She spoke life into my hell that day...and I will forever be grateful.

While it seemed that everything had changed that day, to be honest, nothing changed in my world. Nothing was different after singing that verse. I was the same person at that moment as I had been when standing alone in a crowd just minutes earlier. What changed was not my world but my perspective. I suddenly saw myself through Mrs. Cowan's eyes, and so did my classmates. In her eyes, I was not a loner or loser; I was a singer. From that moment on, I became a singer. Today I am a pastor, but I am still a singer. I am a father of three boys, but I am still a singer. I have a lot of titles today, but I am still a singer. Mrs. Cowan gave me an identity that was not a final point of being; it was actually a starting point for becoming. She changed nothing, except my perspective.

Honestly, the events and words that speak life into our own lives are often not really very profound. When I think back to that morning in chorus, I must admit that Mrs. Cowan's request was not profound. She did not ask me to solve the problem of world hunger. She did not utter some phrase that will be forever etched into the stone monuments of human history. She just told me to sing. The effect of that moment was incredibly profound in my life, but the request itself was not. The profound nature of that moment helped me to discover my perception of my own self-worth.

Before that very moment, I had no concept of any personal ability that could even begin to distinguish me from anyone else who surrounded me. Everyone else seemed to have a sense of intrinsic self-worth that I did not feel I possessed or even deserved. Before then, I was nothing more than a faint shadow on a wall—or so I perceived. That moment allowed me the ability to see myself as more. For the first time in years, I saw...

Worth...

Talent...

Ability...

A person.

I finally saw in myself someone who could achieve. From that moment on, my approach to life changed...and for the better.

2

SPEAK ABILITY

"Concentrate on what you can do, not what you can't."
—*Shirley Watson, Robert's mom*

Growth is allowing my abilities to diminish my disabilities.

I was thirteen, and my life started to crash down around me. I was born with cerebral palsy (CP), which, for those of you who are not familiar with it, is a group of disorders that involve the brain and nervous system. It typically affects muscle movement, and although not detected right away, most who have CP are usually born with it. In many families, I would have been simply cared for and kept comfortable and safe. In my family, I was expected to overcome. My parents, Russell and Shirley Watson, were not into allowing their children to make excuses. Granted, living with CP was a pretty tough lifestyle to succeed in, but overcoming it was still an expectation. I was expected to achieve, just like my other siblings. There were four of us, and each one was expected to carry his or her weight. Each had responsibilities, and each had expectations. I was no different. As a child, I could always get away with things just by playing the cute card. Once I batted those adorable, baby-blue eyes, people would just melt and give in to whatever I wanted. But, at the age of thirteen, I was no longer the cute, blue-eyed, handicapped boy everyone found irresistible. I had become an awkward teen with extra challenges. (As if being an awkward teen wasn't enough of a challenge

4

for one person!) I was unable to compete in sports at school, which can be devastating for a teenage boy. Even playing baseball with my family, I couldn't get to home plate without being thrown out. (I always got on base because I was able to hit the ball a long way; I was just too slow to get around all the bases before the ball caught up with me.) Life was admittedly tougher because of my disability, but then again, life is tough for everyone.

I began to hold pity parties for myself. I would sit around and cry about all the things I couldn't do. I would focus on what the other kids could do and feel sorry for myself. These pity parties would hurt my mom greatly. Though I didn't know it at the time, she was feeling the guilt of wondering what more she could have done to prevent my having CP. Although it was in no way her fault, like most mothers, she blamed herself for my disability. This guilt left her with few options. She could have chosen to attempt to compensate for the harm she incorrectly felt she had caused me. Many parents have tried this. Guilt comes following a divorce, an affair, abuse, poverty, or whatever the perceived shortcoming, and the natural inclination of a parent is to compensate, or even overcompensate, for their children's pain. More often than not, this leaves the children feeling insecure and unsure of their abilities. Mom chose the alternative that would help me to grow. She chose to challenge me rather than to enable me. In doing so, she developed within me a mind-set of confidence and capacity.

Here is how it all played out…

One afternoon while sitting on the porch playing, I began to get upset about all the things I couldn't do. I kept telling my mom over and over again what I couldn't do: "I can't ice-skate. I can't play ball. I can't do anything that the other kids do!" Finally, most likely in frustration, she turned and looked at me and said it: "Robert, you need to concentrate on what you can do instead of what you can't." I just sat there like a puppy that doesn't quite understand what he has just heard. I cocked my head a little to one side but didn't respond. I really had nothing to say. She was right, but I wasn't happy about it or even wanting to admit it.

After that conversation, I began to consider all the things I could do. I could get out of the house and go! I didn't have to be trapped at home alone while everyone else was at work or play. I could get out and go. I could visit friends. I could have conversations with others. I could laugh out loud. I could even drive the lawn mower, which gave me the freedom I desired. I could learn things. I could get good grades. Contrary to the opinion of many, my physical limitations had no effect on my mental capacity. I was smart. There was much to learn, and I had the ability to learn it. Why should I waste time feeling sorry for myself when I could invest time in learning? I didn't have to be alone in my pity parties anymore. In fact, I didn't have to be alone. I could make friends. If *I* needed friends, then other people probably needed friends, too. I could be that friend. I became determined. I became focused. At that point, the things I couldn't do began to take a backseat to the things I could do.

This was a monumental life point. Let's deal with a harsh truth here: we are all disabled. Life has dealt all of us some monumental blows that have undoubtedly left marks on our existence and our psyches. Some of our handicaps are physical. Like me, some bodies just don't physically function as well as others. Yet, some of our handicaps are emotional. Like Mike was, we're convinced that the world has nothing for us but pain and insults. Either way, you've been saddled with limitations that threaten your ability to achieve. Those limitations have the ability to hold you back, but only if you let them. They can only hinder you for as long as you are focused on them. That's right, it just hit some of you: we spend too much time focused on our *dis*abilities and too little time focused on our *cap*abilities.

You see, when I am focused on my disabilities, I find myself getting discouraged and depressed. There is nothing uplifting about focusing on what I cannot do. However, if I focus on what I can do and make it my goal to get even better at doing what I know I can already do, then I find myself encouraged and motivated. The excitement and fulfillment that comes from achievement will drive my life forward. Rather than living in the drag of my disabilities, I can, and should, live in the momentum of my capabilities. Both Mike and I are prime examples of this truth lived out. While neither of us intentionally set out to be examples of this point, as God would have it, we are.

With all of my physical challenges, I've founded or directed numerous national and multinational organizations. I've traveled to various countries and visited places in those countries that would be a physical challenge for anyone, not just someone with cerebral palsy. My refusal to focus on what I can't do has opened many doors of opportunity and paved the way for many experiences that, on the surface, would not have seemed feasible or reasonable. "You can't go to remote villages in Guatemala with cerebral palsy! How are you going to get your scooter around?" But I did. "You can't go visit ancient sites in Israel with cerebral palsy! There are no ramps there!" But I did.

Despite his struggles with insecurity, Mike now finds himself leading the congregation of a large church. He sits with community leaders and works toward solutions for community problems. He serves on numerous boards, from local to international in scope, and influences leaders on a regular basis. His refusal to focus on his emotional scars has opened many doors of opportunity and paved the way for achievements that he otherwise would never have experienced. "You can't get up there and say anything to all those people! What if they don't like you or what you have to say?" But he did. "You can't go in there and meet with that group! They are important people. Who are you?" But he did.

With that said, let's deal with another mistake people make here. Disabilities should not be ignored. They are real. Some people will simply try to ignore their disabilities and hope that they will go away. This is just not realistic. My cerebral palsy is real. Mike's emotional scars are real. These disabilities still exist today. Success does not negate them. Age does not erase them. No amount of prestige or money will make them go away. They are forever a part of whom we are. They cannot, and they must not, be ignored.

Going back to my story, you may have noticed that when I talked about baseball, the issue was my inability to reach home plate. Cerebral palsy, while leaving me with many physical challenges, also has made me exceptionally strong. When I swing a baseball bat, you do not want to be in the way of the ball! I could hit that ball a country mile. Then I would need to get up, take hold of my walker, and tiptoe to first base. I almost always made it to first base, but somewhere between first and second base, the outfield would catch up to me. Sometimes my siblings would feel sorry for me, so they'd throw the ball twenty feet above the second baseman's head. They were doing this to be caring and helpful. It just never worked. Besides being guilty of poor acting (if they had thrown it just barely out of reach, it would have been more believable), they were guilty of being unintentionally insulting. "Since Robert can't do it on his own, we will change the rules just for him." That is virtually never a good idea and almost never helpful. In fact, it can cause much more harm than good.

Anyone with any normal level of mental capacity is aware of his or her own disability. To ignore them or act like they don't exist borders on insulting. The goal is not to ignore the reality but rather to go beyond the reality of the aches, pains, and inconveniences of our troubles and into the life that exists beyond them.

In our church, there is a deaf ministry. Mike was talking with a deaf woman through an interpreter. He wanted to be politically sensitive, so he used the term "hearing impaired" when referring to her disability. She immediately corrected him: "I am not hearing impaired," she said definitively. "I am deaf." No need to ignore it. No need to dance around it. No need to be held back by it. It is just a reality that needs to be overcome, not ignored.

A recent conversation with a friend who also has cerebral palsy began with the normal five-minute update of her aches, pains, and limitations. Then, after a short pause, I asked a question that may seem illogical to some: "So, how's everything going?" After all that discussion about the difficulty of life with cerebral palsy, there is still more to talk about. There is life past the pain and limitations. Too many times, this truth is ignored. Honestly, we often spend so much of our time and energy trying to be sensitive toward all of our struggles that we never get beyond them. The real blessing of this reality check for me was that it came when I was at the young age of thirteen. Early in life, I dealt with limitations and learned to look beyond them. This allowed me to begin to see my abilities—to see what is possible instead of what is not possible.

In every life, there are disabilities, and there are capabilities. The grand question is where we will place our focus. Simply put, we need to recognize and accept our limitations as a fixed reality in our lives. Then we must see beyond those limitations so that we can get past them and spend most of our time working on our capabilities rather than wallowing in our disabilities. This is the difference between those who overcome and those who do not. One reality check separates those who will be trapped with their limitations and those who will excel with them.

3

SPEAK CHALLENGE

"Do your homework like everyone else."
—Mrs. Young, Robert's ninth-grade teacher

Responsibility is always personal.

As a person with cerebral palsy, I soon learned that I have a type of power over others. Other people, not understanding the abilities that I had, would attempt to do things for me that I was fully capable of doing for myself. At least they would attempt to make things easier. One example is my great-aunt Aline. I would ask my father (who would have nothing to do with this easy-life-because-of-a-disability stuff) if I could go help her hoe the crops we grew on her property instead of working other fields. I did this because I knew what Auntie Aline would do. Within a few minutes of me dragging myself dramatically through that field, she would show up with a plate of cookies, a cold soda, and her own hoe. She would physically pick me up and place me under a shade tree with the soda and cookies, and then she would hoe the field. I would get the credit, but she would do the work.

As the years passed, things changed. I went from being a cute little crippled boy with blue eyes (back in the day, "crippled boy" was the common label) to being an awkward teen with a scraggly peach-fuzz beard. If you can imagine all of the normal clumsiness of a thirteen-to-fifteen-year-old boy punctuated by a cerebral palsy limp and a walker with two wheels in the front and metal skis welded to the back (again, back in the day, there were not many advances in assistance tools for the disabled), then you would understand the description from my friends that fit best. According to them, I looked like a scarecrow walking in the wind. So, naturally, I expected most people to underestimate my abilities. Realizing this, I would work the situation to my advantage to get out of some homework assignments. I also was allowed to leave class five minutes early, and the teachers would send a *helper* with me, which made me the most popular kid in class five minutes before the bell. This was all working out just grand.

Then I ran headlong into Mrs. Young. It seemed that Mrs. Young was in charge of facilitating the transition of incoming students with disabilities who were being mainstreamed from a special-needs setting to the regular school setting. Not only that but she had a niece who I knew nothing of and who had a very similar case of cerebral palsy. Needless to say, she had a very different view of my abilities. Mrs. Young also was my English teacher. One afternoon in class, she had everyone begin their English homework. This work was to be handwritten. Now, I had convinced other teachers that, due to my disability, I should not be required to do assignments that involved handwriting. It would certainly take too long and be too difficult. Most of them fell for it, but not Mrs. Young. She walked to my desk and said, "Robby, you need to start your homework." I replied, "No, ma'am, I don't have to do handwriting in any of my other classes." She then replied, "This is my class, and you will do the work." Now, this did not sit well with me because I did not want to do the work. After a few moments of what I considered to be intelligent verbal discussion (I argued), I felt that I was not getting my point across, so to illustrate my frustration, I pushed my books off the desk and onto the floor with a great crash. At that point, Mrs. Young simply bent over, picked up the books, set them back on my desk, and said, "You will do the work." I, again, felt that I was not getting my point across effectively, so I repeated the previous action with another great crash. Again, she picked up the books and, with more authority than the last time, assured me that I was capable of doing the work. After one more display of teenage angst, she looked at me and suggested that she call my parents. Now, having grown up with a very healthy understanding of respecting my elders and the consequences of failure to do so, I asked Mrs. Young not to call my parents. Then she said it: "You will sit there and do your homework like everyone else." "Yes ma'am," I replied…and so I began to struggle with handwriting my homework. (Side note: It really was difficult! I had never faked the difficulty of handwriting; I would just use it to my advantage.)

This little exchange taught me a great lesson. There will always be people who understand my full potential and demand that I reach it. They may be difficult, but they make me a better person. As much as I loved my auntie, she was not helping me grow. Mrs. Young was helping me excel, and ultimately, she helped me to remove barriers. You see, my willingness to allow my disability to become a shortcut was a great danger to my ultimate potential. If I spent my entire life taking shortcuts, I would never grow or develop properly. I would never learn what I needed to learn. I would eventually stop taking risks that seemed too difficult. I would eventually give in to my disabilities and fail to fully develop my abilities.

That would have been tragic.

Yet I see it every day. While no legitimate disability should be overlooked or diminished, neither should any disability be used as a crutch. Honestly, we all have things that hold us back. We all have tasks that are truly difficult to accomplish. While mine was handwriting, yours may have been math. Others may struggle with reading or comprehension, history, or retention of information…the list goes on. The question is not whether you have an area of difficulty in your life; the question is whether you are going to give in to it or work to improve it.

Now, I'm still no good at handwriting, but I haven't allowed that to get the best of me. I may be the only one who can read my writing, but I haven't let that struggle limit my potential. The lesson that Mrs. Young helped me learn is simple: while I may not be in charge of what limits me, I am absolutely in charge of how much I allow myself to be limited.

In the end, handwriting became less of an issue as computers became more prevalent and typing grew to be the accepted way of communication. Today I rarely need to take up a pen and try to write. As so often happens over time, limitations seem to diminish in importance as long as you don't allow them to overtake you. In learning to overcome smaller limitations, you learn that you're able to overcome the larger ones. Once that lesson is learned, limitations become little more than challenges that life dares us to beat. Even difficult, chronic, or lifelong challenges can help us develop if we don't let them overtake us.

So, take the advice of my ninth-grade teacher, and "do your homework like everyone else."

4

SPEAK HONOR

"I don't care what you do with my advice, as long as you listen to it."
—*Clyde Watson, Robert's grandfather*

To listen…to hear…is to learn and grow.

When you are growing up in the country, Friday nights can get a little boring, especially when your friends, brothers, and sisters are out doing things that you are not quite capable of doing yourself. So, I would come up with a solution that would at least get me out of the house. I would secretly call my grandmother. I would ask her to call my mom to invite me over for the evening. You see, Mom thought it was rude to go over to grandmother's without an invitation. In no time at all, there I was, hanging out with my grandparents. Now this might not seem like much excitement to you, but remember, this was country life, and I was out of the house! We would play games, watch television, and talk. During these talks, I learned a great deal from my grandparents.

One Friday night, my grandfather was pondering some point he thought was important for me to learn. He was a very wise man and had much he wanted to teach me. Honestly, I've been blessed with a great family, and there was much wisdom to be gained from my parents and grandparents. Anyway, I must have seemed a bit disinterested in the point that Grandfather was making, because he stopped and gave me a hard stare. He then looked over the rim of his glasses and cleared his throat to make sure he had my attention. Then he said it: "I don't care what you do with my advice, as long as you listen to it."

At first I was a little taken aback. I didn't mean to insult my grandfather; I just wasn't interested at the moment. Then I thought about what he had said. He was right. It didn't matter how I chose to apply his wisdom; it mattered that I heard it. Simply put, we can't learn from anything we don't hear. We can't apply anything we haven't learned, and we can't grow from anything we haven't applied. So it's very important that we learn to listen to those who would take the time to speak wisdom and truth—speak life—into our lives.

Honestly, some of the best advice will often come from what seems to be the least interesting at the time. Therefore, the challenge is to learn the art of listening. You see, God made gold hard to find. If gold were easy to find, then it would not be valuable. It would be just another rock. Instead, gold is rare and difficult to find. Even when found, it is difficult to extract. Even extracted, it is difficult to refine.

Truth is like gold.

On the surface, there may be no indication that gold nuggets exist underground. On the surface, we may see only tranquil pastures or even difficult, rugged rock with no indication of what lies beneath. We have all met these people—the quiet, tranquil pastureland of a grandparent who seems to float through our lives with barely a ripple of evidence that they were even there. They have no desire to stir up our lives or bring attention to themselves. We've met others who have been left ragged and rock hard from the battles of a difficult life. It's not comfortable to be with these ragged and hard people. In fact, they seem angry and almost dangerous at times, which may not be a real indication of what lies just beneath their surface.

Gold can be found under most all surfaces if you're willing to dig for it. I think that's one of the great differences between people who find wisdom and those who do not. It seems that most people are not really willing to dig for nuggets of truth. They satisfy themselves with the pretty rocks they find lying around that are easily accessible, and they never experience the pure gold of a discovered nugget of real truth.

They seem to think that discovering truth is just too difficult. Others have argued that such nuggets of truth don't even exist. They suggest that nothing beneath the surface can be all that meaningful. Their mentality is to just do their thing and not worry about finding truth and relevance. Just have fun.

While gathering the common, pretty rocks or just forgetting to search for gold nuggets, each have their own allure, and both leave a person feeling empty. Life without the gold nuggets of truth is hardly worth living.

To live without truth is to live without meaning and purpose.

To live without truth is to live without hope and direction.

To live without truth is not really living at all; it is simply existing.

Too many people simply exist.

These people exist adrift on the random currents of daily life left to the uncaring, undirected, and heartless hands of fate. While this idea may seem, at least on the surface, to be freeing and easy, it actually leads to fear and despair. Without truth, meaning, direction, and hope, there can be no peace, security, drive, joy, or real reason to live. Those who reject the importance or existence of truth are wrong.

Truth does exist; it's worthwhile, and it can be found...even behind the eyes of a grandparent...behind the anger of a parent...behind the devotion of a child...or behind the embrace of a lover.

Just behind the heart of every human being is an ethereal, elusive element that cannot be studied, extracted, held or seen: the soul. Nuggets of truth reside in the deep caverns of a person's soul. They sit there, waiting to be found, waiting to be mined, and waiting to be heard. God put them there. The very creator of our body and soul knew that there must be more to us than the physical. So, he, in an ultimate step of divine wisdom, placed a soul deep within us and then filled it with the nuggets of truth that those around us desperately need to find. Then, in a step of pure genius, he placed within us an unquenchable desire to find and reveal those very truths.

Brilliant!

The problem is, though, that we don't always want to listen. Like I was on that Friday night with my grandfather, we are disinterested.

Preoccupied. Busy. Overwhelmed. Tired. Angry. We don't feel like mining truth most of the time. It just doesn't seem worth it. But truth is always worth the effort because it grows us. It expands our understanding of everything around and within us. It overcomes our narrow thinking and challenges our shallow living. Truth expands our very lives. Truth must be sought. Truth must be found. Truth must be applied.

This brings us back to that Friday night with my grandfather. What he told me that night didn't seem particularly important at the moment. In fact, I still couldn't tell you the advice he imparted to me before he uttered that one statement that I will never forget. However, I can tell you this: I have never received a useless truth. Somewhere, somehow, truth is always useful. It may not seem like it at the moment, but a gold nugget always comes in handy. In fact, gold nuggets are heavy and difficult to carry. The weight of a great truth can sit heavy and hard on our shoulders, but it's always worth carrying. A day will come when the application of that nugget will be a lifesaver. So, just store it, and carry it. Even the nuggets that seem irrelevant or too small to worry about add up. In the end, our worth is measured in these nuggets of truth we gather and apply. Our character is built on such truths. Our reputation is built on our character. The legacy we leave behind is built on our reputation and character. So what will you do with all the advice you receive? Honestly, I don't care, as long as you listen to it!

5

SPEAK BEAUTY

"Someday that will make a beautiful homesite."
—Russell Watson, Robert's dad

Beauty is found beneath the weeds.

It was a beautiful spring afternoon, and I was home from college for the weekend. It was one of those afternoons where you suddenly find a few extra minutes of free time. Dad and I were talking, and he was telling me about a property he had just bought. Having grown up on the farm, my brothers, sisters, and I had explored almost every inch of Dad's land, and a good bit of the neighbors' properties as well. I was familiar with the place he had bought, and I knew it to be pretty much just a gully full of trees. Dad seemed somehow excited about this place; he seemed to see something in it that I just didn't quite see. In fact, he had already started digging out a pond in the gully of trees. Finally, he said to me, "Robert, let's go christen the pond!" Well, I knew what that meant. Dad wanted us to return some of the water we had so greedily taken from nature, if you know what I mean. Of course, it sounded like a great idea to me. So off we went.

Parked in his truck at the bottom of what was one day to be a pond, Dad began to describe what his mind saw. He saw a beautiful pond, a duck-hunting blind, a fishing dock, a grassy hill, a rustic dirt road…and it all sounded so beautiful. Yet, his vision bore no resemblance to what I was seeing. This was a muddy gully full of trees. It just looked like a mess to me. I didn't want to tell Dad that all I saw was a disaster. He seemed to see so much potential. Pointing up at the hill covered with a scraggly forest, he said it: "Robert, someday that will make a beautiful homesite."

What? There? I knew that hill had been destroyed by a tornado some years earlier. That's why the woods were so damaged. I was prepared to reject this damaged place, but again, I didn't say anything. Dad saw something I did not. He was always good at that. He could look over a hill, into a valley, or across a field and see things that just weren't there. He was somehow able to see beneath the weeds and capture what was possible in his mind's eye. He always could do that. He always did that with me.

This ability to see beyond what is and into what could be is a profound gift. Not everyone has it. For many of us, a tree-filled, muddy gully could just never be a beautiful pond. In fact, it could never be anything but a muddy gully. That's all we see, so that's all we think is possible. For some, there is more than meets the eye. Some have the ability to look into that muddy hole in the ground and see geese gathering on the water and children fishing off a dock. Now that's vision. And that's really what this gift is all about. It is the ability to see a person or place as more. We need more people with this gift—this vision. We need them to look over the landscape of our lives and through the weeds and scraggly forest of our jumble of talents, weaknesses, capabilities, disabilities, joys, successes, and failures, to see what is possible.

Too often we allow ourselves to be surrounded by people who do not have this gift of vision. We listen to voices of those who see us as we are at the moment and not as who we could, and arguably should, become. In the jumbled, tangled mess of our daily struggle for existence and acceptance, we need someone with vision to help us see what we sometimes fail to recognize. When our eyes are open, we have hope. God places these people with vision in our lives to speak the very truth we need...the very truth he knows we need. These very people can help us get beyond the mess in our lives to the beauty that lies just beneath the weeds. With that said, we need to understand this: perception is reality. Most people will never look hard enough to see if there is more to you than what they immediately perceive. For them, that perception is reality.

The problem comes when we buy into that way of thinking. When we allow the perceptions of ourselves to be driven by those who have not made any effort to consider what is possible in our lives, we fall victim to the tyranny of small expectations. Potential is lost to a perception that is narrow, limited, shallow, and wrong. Someone, somewhere, sometime can help us look into our lives and see more.

Once someone has seen more in us, the job really begins. Many of us tend to lean toward the negative when it comes to self-assessment. We see the problems, shortcomings, and failures, and we tend to focus on them. This limits our perspective. Taken to the extreme, this limitation of perspective can leave us alone, depressed, and hopeless. This path can lead to self-destructive behavior—even suicide—if it is not addressed. This path will destroy us instead of building us. In fact, as counterintuitive as it may seem, this path leads to self-absorption. We become so lost in our perceived inabilities that we actually don't see anyone or anything else. Our own pain, our own failure, our own hopelessness closes in on our minds and crowds out any thought of anyone or anything else. Yet, if someone plants a seed of hope in us, it can make all the difference. When someone else looks into our lives and sees potential that we did not think was there and then takes the time to convince us that they are right, they can change the entire trajectory of our lives.

This change requires work on our part. For us to see the potential that lies beneath the weeds in our own lives, we must allow visionaries to cut down the scraggly forest that defines our perception of ourselves. They must be willing to invest the time and energy to painstakingly help us clear the landscape and see the potential. We, in turn, must be willing to invest the time and endure the pain of uprooting our false personal assumptions. These weeds of doubt that cover up our potential often have been planted over many years. Insults, failures, successes, and rejections all play a role in the growth of this field of weeds on top of what should be our field of dreams.

This is why positive visionaries are so important in our lives. As they help us to remove the weeds, they continue to encourage our development. They implant a sense of hope and direction in our lives. They convince us that we're capable of doing and becoming more. On the other hand, if we surround ourselves with the weed planters, they will work just as hard. Their work is different; it is easier. They simply need to scatter seeds of doubt. No cultivating is necessary. Just toss out a few negative thoughts and demeaning situations, and it's amazing how fast those weeds of self-doubt grow. Surrounding ourselves with positive visionaries increases our potential, while being with weed planters diminishes it. Both are convincing and powerful, but only visionaries make us better than we currently are.

Now, vision alone does not produce results. That muddy gully was nothing more. It was not as if some magical place was hidden just beneath all those weeds. No, there was potential, but the magic was in the work. That gully had to be cleaned out. The scraggly woods had to be cut down and cleaned up. The hunting shed and fishing dock had to be built. The pond had to be stocked. The house needed to be built. The yard needed to be laid out, leveled up, and sown with grass. Landscaping had to be done, and a road had to be established. Until all of that took place, nothing was there but a muddy gully.

In the same way, we must recognize that our lives require work. When the weed planters speak into our lives, they are most often not being dishonest. They are speaking to a reality that exists. They have looked at us, seen our flaws, pointed them out, and reminded us how they will limit us. Again, they are right, but that only speaks to my current reality. It overlooks my future potential. Likewise, when the positive visionaries speak into our lives, they too are not being dishonest. They have looked at us and seen our flaws and understand how we can be limited...but they see more. The difference here is not in how these two individuals have defined us. The difference is in what these two would do with us from this point forward.

Let's be completely honest; the weed planters offer the path of least resistance, and to allow their view of reality to prevail, I don't need to do a single thing. I just sit back and accept the limitations. No work required.

The positive visionaries, on the other hand, offer us a lengthy to-do list. There are hills to be cleared, trees to be cut, ponds to be dug, docks to be built, a house to be designed, and the list goes on and on. It seems that the work never ends. In fact, it doesn't. Personal development is hard, never-ending work, but it will develop within us a new and better reality. With the encouragement of a positive visionary, the work can get done. We can be more.

So what about that scraggly hill overlooking that muddy gully? Well, Dad was right. It made a beautiful homesite. Today I sit in my office and look down over that pond. I look down over the duck-hunting shed and dock reflected in the calm, clear water. The mirror is occasionally disrupted by the splash and ripple of a jumping fish or the landing of a few geese. What was once only a dream in my Dad's mind is now a stunning reality.

Now I see it.

Sometimes I wonder if Dad feels the same way about me. Has he looked over the weed-covered scraggly hill of his son's life and saw more. He worked that hill every day of my life. He pulled weeds that could have left me feeling rejected and failed. He planted confidence that allowed me to take on challenges that others would have called insurmountable. He planted the love and security that only comes from knowing that someone will always be there. Thank God for a man of vision. Thank God my Dad looked at me and saw more.

Now I see it.

6

SPEAK LEGACY

"Be careful where you walk; someone may follow in your footsteps."
—*Geneva Boyd, Robert's college friend*

Influence is a great gift that can be nurtured or squandered.

While I was in college, I dated a girl named Geneva. She gave me a gift that I have kept to this day. It was a very simple needlepoint containing the following words: "Be careful where you walk; someone may follow in your footsteps." At first glance, I saw nothing more than a cute needlepoint, and I was just flattered that she had spent time sewing it for me. The phrase itself did not really catch me at the time. However, over the years, I have come to realize the power in those simple words. Honestly, it is a great line.

This needlepoint has become a constant reminder of the care with which influence must be wielded. As we grow in our lives, careers, families, and reputation, we must understand that our circle of influence increases. Others begin to watch what we do and how we react, and they take note of and even emulate us. Here is where influence gets scary. When we are young and unknown, our decisions only affect a small circle of people, and we may feel that we can do what we want and not worry much about what others think. When others start paying closer attention and taking note of what we do, we must be very careful.

You see, our lives are like beacons along a dark waterway. As others are trying to navigate areas that we have already traveled, they use our experiences and decisions as guideposts on their own journey. When we choose poorly, most people instinctively know not to follow our direction. Most will see our poor decisions and the damage caused, and they will avoid our mistakes. However, some will not learn from our mistakes. Due to the relationship we have with them or to their lack of discernment, they will simply follow our path to their own disastrous end. Those same people who follow our decisions, no matter how dangerous or destructive they may be, are likely to follow our good choices as well. In everything we do, we must deal with the fact that someone is watching us. Someone is following us. We must realize that, as we grow in our lives, our field of influence grows. This means that even more people are affected by our decisions. We simply must deal with the fact that, eventually, others learn from and repeat our actions. We can cause great damage if we are not thoughtful with our decisions.

In southern Maryland, there are two great soaring birds. Both can float aloft on the winds for what seems like hours. Both are impressive in size. Both are well known. Though that is where the similarity ends. One of these birds is common. It is seen every day, hovering, resting, or eating all around the area. The other is somewhat rare, seen only occasionally, and always noted upon its arrival. One elicits emotions that range from nausea to fear, while the other elicits emotions of pride and freedom.

The first is a buzzard. They are very common here. On any given day, you will observe them circling in the sky or gorging themselves on some poor, helpless creature who ended up in the wrong road at the wrong time. Just the image of these buzzards circling seems to indicate imminent death. (This is all right, I guess, as long as they are not circling over me.) These birds, while important to the overall balance of nature, are anything but revered. Their habits are disgusting. Their diet is disgusting. Their appearance is disgusting. Their reputation is horrible. Yet they do have one advantage over all other large birds: there are tons of them. At times, dozens of them gather on radio towers or in trees. In some neighborhoods, they tend to congregate in large numbers and perch on the roofs of homes and in the woods behind these homes. These birds are so disliked that they can actually lower the market value of a house if too many are around. That is part of the problem with buzzards; there are always more than enough of them around. In fact, there is never a lack of buzzards looking for a way to capitalize on the misfortune of others.

Sadly, people can be like that. We all have come across those who seem to hover around, looking for an opportune moment to take advantage of some unsuspecting soul. They wait for the struggles of life to become more than someone can bear and then feed off of those who are too weak to continue. Or they sit by the highways of life and wait. Here, they wait for those crushing, unexpected moments when a huge problem approaches us at blinding speed and suddenly knocks the life right out of us. They linger. They wait for the pain and death of our trauma to bring the rotting stench of disillusionment or despair and then swoop in for their putrid feast. We may see people like this as disgusting and vile, but they are not rare. They are, unfortunately, all too common.

The second bird is the bald eagle. Eagles are majestic. They are beautiful. They are powerful. They are capable hunters. They are revered. They are rare. Many people go through their entire lives and never see one in the wild. When we do see them, we pause. We point them out. We stand and watch as they majestically soar over the earth with grace, elegance, and freedom. People love to see eagles. I remember watching one of these wonderful creatures soar over the Potomac River while standing on the porch at Mount Vernon. This symbol of strength and freedom soared past the house that was once occupied by a man who envisioned both strength and freedom for an entire nation. This bird, like this man, was a rare treasure.

This majestic bird, though rare, is becoming more common here in southern Maryland. There are reasons for this. In our reverence for the eagle, we have put in place certain protections for them. We have decided that their presence among us is important enough to merit special treatment and restrictions. We have been working to maintain a healthy habitat in which the birds can live and flourish. Our goal is not to disturb the family units that produce and train the young. We strive to help the eagle survive and thrive.

There are people who could be described as eagles. These are the rare folks who seem to be able to soar above their circumstances and majestically overcome the obstacles that the rest of us labor to simply endure. These are the few who are capable of instilling in us a desire for more. They raise their mighty wings and inspire us by the sheer power of the wind they can generate as they lift off for yet another great flight. They awaken within us our own desire to soar above life's struggles, if only for a moment, and to capture an eagle's view of the road ahead. These people inspire us to be more than we believe we can be. These people are eagles. These people are rare.

The truth is that every one of us must make a decision in our lives between being a common buzzard or a rare eagle. In the words of my dad, "If you want to soar with the eagles, you cannot hang around with the buzzards." Simply put, eagles hang with eagles. That's how they learn to act like an eagle. They learn how to fly, soar, provide, and inspire. None of these lessons are learned from buzzards. None. Hanging with buzzards does me no good if I wish to become an eagle. In fact, it does me great harm. Hanging with buzzards teaches me poor habits and morals. Dining on the rotting and putrid waste of the world around us seems, at first glance, to be something that none of us would ever do. If we spend enough time with buzzards, the rotting, nauseating, putrid meal will begin to smell like fun. Those gathering around a day-old carcass will start to look like a party. The stomach full of rotted flesh will begin to feel like success.

Not a pretty picture? Of course not, but this is where you are headed if you hang with buzzards—and not only you but also those who follow you. All too often I have spoken with parents struggling with their own poor examples and devastated by the resulting unwise decisions of their children. Their children had followed—and followed well. All too often, I have spoken to a leader who struggled with the selfish example he had set for his employees and then lamented the lack of cohesion and caring within his organization. They had followed—and followed well. All too often, I have sat with pastors who struggled with their own difficult and overbearing example they set for their congregation and were then crushed by the lack of love and compassion within their church. They had followed—and followed well. Honestly, most people are great followers. Only a few are great leaders. Just a few can move beyond feeding off the failure of others and begin to nurture others' desire to be more.

The application here is actually simple. We must make good decisions in our lives so that we can be good examples to those around us. We must live lives that produce eagles out of those who choose to emulate us. We must be careful where and how we walk because, eventually, someone just might follow in our footsteps.

7

SPEAK VISION

"Jump, Preacher!"
—*Dan Bouch, church treasurer, New Life Church*

Faith beyond self produces courage beyond fear.

I t was just one of those meetings that every leader dreads. I had only been the pastor of New Life Church for a couple of years, and while things were going pretty well, there were big decisions on the horizon. As a fairly new leader in this growing congregation, I was proposing yet another aggressive hiring and expansion budget. I was keenly aware of the risk of continuously stretching the edges of nonprofit growth potential and of the dangers involved in losing momentum. So here we were, caught between the need for stability and the need for growth.

While most people don't recognize it, growth creates instability. It's a type of instability we are comfortable with, because growth is often our goal—but it is nonetheless unstable. The instability of growth can bring insecurity and fear for a board of leaders who haven't been accustomed to the frightening feeling of this ever-changing reality. So that night, I was approaching the board with gentleness and compassion. Honestly, I was as nervous as they were. For them, the stakes were high. Their church was on the line. The place where they worshipped, the place they found meaning, and the place where they wanted their children and grandchildren to find God was suddenly and completely changing.

In fact, though we didn't realize it at the time, we were planning the funeral of the church for which they had worked so hard at growing and maintaining. You see, as any organization grows, it inevitably changes. Once the organization has changed enough, what used to be is no more. Truth be told, the church we were talking about that night ceased to exist—due, in large part, to the decisions we made that very night. Their church was literally on the line.

For me, it was compounded one step further. Not only was my church on the line but also my career. My family's financial stability was certainly in play. To make an aggressive move and succeed seems brilliant to the world around you. To make an aggressive move and fail seems foolish. There isn't much middle ground in this. It's a Charlie Brown moment. You will either be the hero or the goat. Few churches hire used-up goats. So my career was on the line that night. In fact, if I am to be completely honest, as a leader of a nonprofit organization, my family's financial stability is in play each and every time we make a risky decision. The only real variable in most nonprofit budgets is staffing, and though I may be the last to go, I am the first to take a pay cut. So I entered into that discussion with the respect, humility, and fear that it demanded.

The board at New Life Wesleyan Church where I am the pastor has always seemed to have more faith than I do. So as I began to try to balance out the potential risks and rewards of moving forward with such an aggressive plan, they listened and joined the discussion. After some time, the room fell into one of those awkward silences that occur just before the moment when the discussion has probably run its course but everyone is waiting to see if there might be a little more. In that moment, it was Dan Bouch who broke the silence. Now, Dan, or Danny as we call him here, was the treasurer. I had always known him as financially conservative and yet aggressive in ministry. Danny wanted to reach the world, and he was willing to take risks to accomplish that goal. He also wanted the money cared for with the utmost caution and integrity. So I wasn't entirely certain what he was going to say at that moment. Then he came out with a phrase that he has repeated often since. In that awkward, silent moment of decision, Danny simply said, "Jump, Preacher!"

That phrase often rings in my ears, even today, as I face risky and aggressive ministry or business decisions. On the precipice of risk, I almost always hear Danny's voice: "Jump, Preacher!" And let me tell you, for a guy who is naturally afraid of heights, the imagery is vivid! My fear of heights is almost matched by my aversion to risk. I wasn't raised to take risks. I was taught to grow up, get a good stable job, avoid risk, and live a nice quiet life. Well, I have never been very good at that, but I do still have a natural aversion to risk. Danny helped me to overcome my fear that night, and in many ways, he is still helping me to overcome my fears today.

If it can help people who need help: "Jump, Preacher!"

If it's not all about you: "Jump, Preacher!"

If there is a reasonable expectation of success: "Jump, Preacher!"

If it is best in the long run, even though difficult now: "Jump, Preacher!"

If God is in it: "Jump, Preacher!"

I still have one question. Where does a conservative treasurer come up with that kind of advice? Anyone who has served on the leadership board of a nonprofit can tell you that the treasurer is the last one to be open to risk. It's the money guy who is sounding the alarm warnings against risk, and rightly so. The treasurer is the one charged with long-term stability. It's the treasurer's job to make certain that the organization can pay its bills, meet its obligations, and survive. Risk is not exactly the treasurer's friend. So why was Danny so confident? Where did this willingness to take a risk come from?

Danny's confidence actually speaks to a profound truth in any type of organizational growth or leadership. Any organization, any person for that matter, is moving in some direction in an attempt to arrive at some destination. There is a sense of movement within the life of a healthy person or organization. Someone or something must guide this movement.

In a business, the driving force is financial.

In a nonprofit organization, the driving force is benevolence.

In a government, the driving force is societal.

In a church, the driving force is spiritual.

Whatever the driving force of the organization may be, it must be present, and it must be maintained. In fact, when that driving force ceases to exist, the organization is doomed to failure and, ultimately, extinction. When that force is clearly seen, clearly understood, reasonably applied, and carefully maintained, the organization can see phenomenal growth and effectiveness. It was this driving force to which Danny was reacting.

As a leader, I was caught up in a fear that perhaps I didn't have what it would take to move the church forward. I was worried about my own abilities and inabilities. Danny wasn't thinking about that. In fact, though it might sound harsh, Danny wasn't thinking about me at all. The thought that New Life Church would be fine because I was a great leader never crossed Danny's mind. He was reacting to something larger. He was acting in faith because he believed in what God was doing. You see, the driving force in the church is the presence and power of God. Certainly there are great leaders in the church, but they are not the driving force. It is God that empowers and moves forward his church. We, as leaders, just act and react to his presence and movement. Danny saw that...and I suppose my fear exposes the fact that I did not. The treasurer taught the pastor a lesson about faith. While I was worried about my own future and career, he was focused on the mission we had signed up to carry out.

We were reaching people, and that was what we were there to do, so let's keep it up!

While this is working, let's work it.

Don't slow down when you are making progress; if at all possible, speed up.

Now, none of these last three statements makes any sense at all if I am simply focused on my own abilities and strengths. In fact, there are a lot of limitations to my strengths and abilities. There are also many limitations to yours. We can only take our dreams so far on our own. Even in a group, we can only go so far. Every organization and every person needs something else. We all need something that calls us to operate outside our normal limits of giftedness, even if only for a while.

I grew up in North Carolina. Being from that state has a few requirements. You need to love barbecue, sweet tea, and basketball. So for most of my life, I remember watching some team from my home state playing in the NCAA Championship Tournament. Over the years, it was great fun watching UNC Chapel Hill, Duke, and Wake Forest win championships and pretty much force the rest of the county to travel North Carolina roads if they ever hoped to be anybody in college basketball. But in all those great moments, there is one that stands above all the others. Everyone expects Chapel Hill and Duke to compete for a national title every year, so at the start of the 1983 ACC Tournament, it was expected that the Tar Heels and Blue Devils would once again play for the championship. However, there was another team quietly gaining some steam that no one had noticed. Jimmy Valvano coached NC State at the time. He had convinced his players that they could play with these big boys and win. And win they did. In a shocking turn of events, they won the ACC Tournament that year and, with it, gained an automatic invitation to the NCAA Tournament. Without that championship, they would not have been invited.

So here you have this Cinderella team out of North Carolina that happens to pull off a great weekend and win the ACC Tournament. No big deal, right? You see, that was the problem. No one thought the streak would continue...but it did. Game after game, this team outperformed expectations and won. Finally, the national championship game was here, and the North Carolina State University Wolfpack was playing the Houston Cougars, a team with such talent that they were ranked number one and had been dubbed Phi Slamma Jamma. No one was supposed to beat these guys. Here is where strength from outside yourself comes in. The NC State Wolfpack was now completely convinced that they would win.

No one else was.

They were not talented enough.

They were not tall enough.

They were not strong enough.

They were not deep enough.

Yet they were convinced enough.

They had a confidence in something beyond their own ability. That confidence did not come from their talent. Everyone knew Houston was more talented, but that did not matter. That confidence did not come from a great winning record. Everyone knew that Houston had a better record, but that did not matter. That confidence came from somewhere else, but not from deep inside them as much as from somewhere around and outside of them. Something else was pushing them. Something else was empowering them. This was their year, although they were the only ones who knew it.

Certainly momentum can be generated internally. We can push ourselves and our organization forward by our own sheer will to succeed. Certainly we can create systems and plans that will push us forward—sometimes at an amazing pace.

But miracles don't happen there.

Miracles happen when momentum gains a life of its own. Miracles happen when we stop trying to convince others of our abilities and the momentum itself begins to convince us. At that point, it can sweep you and those around you to newer and higher places than you thought possible. That is what happened to the Wolfpack in the spring of 1983. Many have told this story and relived the wonder of such an unlikely ride. Many have asked themselves what propelled a team with less talent and potential to such great heights. Many have tried to contain or explain this phenomenon, but none have succeeded. We just can't manufacture those kinds of results. There was something else at play there. Call this *something else* whatever you wish. Call it faith. Call it fate. Call it destiny. Just don't ignore it, because to do so would be a grave mistake. Just ask the University of Houston. By the way, the Wolfpack won 54-52 on a last-second shot! Welcome to basketball in North Carolina.

So what does all this have to do with Danny and his jump-preacher statement? It's simple really. Too often we fail to succeed at the highest levels because we simply rely on our own ability and strength. We limit ourselves to what is possible, reasonable, or expected, and in doing so, we ignore the powerful reality that exists outside of us. We ignore the driving forces around us that could take us higher and further than we ever imagined. Call it what you will, this something else is powerful.

It's no secret that Robert and I are both Christians. We believe in the presence and power of the Holy Spirit of God. We believe that this

Holy Spirit can carry us to places unimaginable on our own. We believe in a strength that can be found in God's presence and that far outpaces our own strengths. It is in that strength—his strength—that decisions can be made with confidence—even risky ones. Even when it seems that everything is on the line and failure would lead to certain doom, his power is greater. That is what Danny was talking about.

Danny's faith was not in me.

Danny's faith was not in our church.

Danny's faith was not in our board.

Danny's faith was in our God.

When that reality struck me, I chose. I chose to be aggressive. I chose to take risk. I chose to believe. It wasn't such a hard thing to do. I wasn't choosing to believe in me. That wouldn't work. I know me too well. I was choosing to believe in something else...I was choosing to believe in God. Therefore, I could take greater risks because I was operating with a greater power. I could go further because I was operating with more. Simply put, I could have faith because I was moving in a current that I did not create, empower, or manage. I was just supposed to ride.

By the way, we made those aggressive and risky decisions that night, and the results have been simply amazing.

Still scary? You bet.

Worthwhile? Absolutely!

So look for it. Look for a moment when that something else in your life is on the move. Seek it out...and when you find it...jump!

8

SPEAK LEADERSHIP

"You can take this organization to places we cannot imagine."
—*Lucy Waletzky, Robert's boss and founder/president of Dateable*

The faith of others releases untapped potential.

I n 1988, I met my wife, Lynn Robertshaw, at a Valentine's Day party organized by a group called Dateable. This group specializes in combating isolation among people in the disabled community and offers a forum for dating relationships to develop. Well, in our case, it worked. Although I showed up to that event ninety-three minutes late, Lynn still found me interesting and eventually married me in 1992. She is truly a patient woman.

Following that Valentine's Day party, I became more involved in Datable and eventually was asked to join the board of directors. In 1991, I asked Lynn to marry me. About two months before our April wedding, the founder and CEO of Dateable, Lucy Waletzky, invited us to New York for the filming of a cable show about Dateable. We were to be the featured couple on the show. As we all traveled back from the taping to Washington, DC, where we lived, I began to share my vision for the future of Dateable with Lucy. All that had been churning in my heart and mind over the past year on the board of directors just flowed out into our conversation. Lucy just listened.

Three days later, I received a call from Lucy. She began to refer back to our conversation on the way home from New York. She wondered if I thought my projections for the future of Dateable were realistic. I assured her that I thought they were. Two days after that conversation, Lucy called back. This time she asked me to put the entire plan into writing. I wasn't certain what she was going to do with my ideas, but she was interested in them, and I was flattered. So I wrote them all down for her, and one week later, Lucy called again. This time she had a proposition. She asked if I would be interested in becoming the executive director of Dateable. My head spun a bit as I considered the opportunity. I had not expected this. I was not presenting this five-year plan as a pitch for a job. I just thought it was a good idea. Anyway, I already had a good job. My job already allowed me to speak on behalf of those with cerebral palsy on a regular basis. It was stable, and I was happy. Yet this was a great opportunity. Lucy could sense my hesitancy, and she began to encourage me. She liked the plan I had articulated. She saw the same potential in Dateable that I saw. During that conversation, she said one thing in particular that caught my attention, which was, "You can take this organization to places we cannot imagine."

With that, I was sold. I went back and talked to Lynn, and we decided together that it was the right thing to do. I quit my job and became the executive director of Dateable. Honestly, I made this decision based less on my faith in my own plan and more because of Lucy's faith in me.

On a side note, I had established three goals that I intended to reach before I turned thirty: get married, own my own home, and run my own organization. On April 10, 1992, Lucy allowed me to reach one of these goals by naming me the executive director of Dateable. On April 18, 1992, Lynn and I were married and moved into our own home, accomplishing goals two and three. On April 24, 1992, I celebrated my thirtieth birthday. Lucy, Lynn, and Dateable had opened the door to accomplishing my top three goals as a young man. As celebrations go, it was a wonderful month. As stressors go, I hit three of the top five stressors anyone can face within three weeks: new job, new wife, and new home.

I was ready for the future.

Do not overestimate the power of someone else's confidence. None of us can endure for long or accomplish much with only our own confidence. Eventually faith in ourselves runs out. When that happens, we need the additional boost of someone else's confidence in us. That boost is enough to carry us through the difficult seasons and propel us forward to greater days. In my case, it was Lynn and Lucy who showed so much faith in my abilities. Their confidence gave me confidence.

Now, let's be honest here. I had just been named the executive director of what amounted to a dating service for handicapped persons. Truth be told, I am a lousy matchmaker. I don't enjoy matchmaking, and I am not good at it. What Lucy saw in me, and what I believed about me, was that I was a good networker of people. I may not be able to get two people in the Washington, DC, area to start dating, but I could rally together enough support to take the Dateable program nationwide. Within three years, we accomplished just that. We actually reached every goal stated in our five-year plan in the first three years of effort. What I believed was true of myself, and what Lucy had encouraged in me, was becoming a reality.

Since that time, many things have changed. Over the past seventeen years, Dateable has experienced many transformations. Today, our goal of combating isolation among people with disabilities is being realized through more than just the one program we began in 1992. Today Dateable is an umbrella organization for implementation or cooperation with various programs designed to combat isolation. While we do less matchmaking, we do more to accomplish our main mission nationwide: helping those with disabilities to feel less isolated and more integrated.

This is what I had hoped for.

This is what Lucy believed I could do.

This is what her faith and trust empowered me to accomplish.

Right now, in every person's life, there is a tug-of-war going on between what we are truly capable of and what we are afraid to try. In this battle, the weight of fear pulls heavily against our willingness to try new and challenging things.

Something must counteract that weight.

Someone must counterbalance that fear.

Someone else's confidence must fill in the gaps that our own personal confidence leaves behind.

Someone must speak life into our lives.

Without this kind of support from others, none of us would ever attempt great things. You see, great things are not so much accomplished by great people; rather, convinced people accomplish them. The effectiveness of Dateable and its partner organizations has little to do with my personal skills and abilities. It has more to do with the confidence that Lucy placed in me to gather others together with a similar dream. Her confidence in and spoken to me allowed me to try. Her confidence in me spoken to others allowed them to have faith in me as well. Her confidence in me fueled my willingness to try and my efforts to succeed.

That kind of confidence does not come along often, but it does come. When it does, we must be willing to act on it. To ignore someone's trust placed in us or to fail to act on that trust is to squander the very opportunity that we have all hoped for in our lives. In short, we all start out as small fish in a big pond. We have a couple of choices. We can refuse to grow, becoming little more than food for big fish, or we can act on the faith of others and grow. Eventually we become bigger. One day we look around to find that we are a big fish in a big pond. Not so much because of our talent or greatness but because of someone else's faith in us.

Their faith is fuel we run on. Again, we must realize that our own faith in our own abilities is never sufficient.

It takes others.

It takes encouragement.

It takes a Lucy who will make us believe.

Then the statement becomes a reality. "You can take this organization to places we cannot imagine."

9

SPEAK ENDURANCE

"Wait until you roll up the hill."
— *Chris Bryan, Robert's friend and personal trainer*

Hard work prepares the way for unanticipated joy.

I am approaching forty-seven years old. In the process, I am dealing with aging with cerebral palsy. Honestly, I am very solid and healthy, but I have lost a step or two. You see, as a farm boy, I developed a muscular body that helped me through my high-school years. Because of my strength, I was always able to beat the bullies in arm wrestling. This proved to be extremely effective, because my opponents and their followers would always give me a higher level of respect as they remembered their sore biceps after challenging me. Quite often these arm-wrestling matches actually resulted in lasting friendships.

Over the years, I have done extensive research in cerebral palsy and aging. Depending on the functioning level of a given person, an individual with cerebral palsy ages at a 1:2 or 1:5 ratio as compared to a person without cerebral palsy. So we will assume that I fit into a 1:3 ratio. That would mean that I actually have a body age of approximately sixty-one years old. To be completely honest, before I married Lynn in '92, I was buff, but I gradually gave up lifting weights for lifting utensils.

As the years have passed, I have used my electric scooter more and more. Interestingly, after building an ultra-accessible home in 1998, the situation became even worse. Since the house was equipped with wide-open spaces in order to get around in the scooter, walking was made more difficult, and so my dependence on the scooter grew. While I have always traveled a lot, I began to find it more and more difficult to do so. So when Pastor Mike asked me to go on a mission trip to the Philippines, I questioned if I could commit to the travel. For the most part, the town we were traveling to in the Philippines was not accessible, and the trip to the Philippines itself would require four airplanes and a three-hour van ride on an extremely bumpy road. Nevertheless, I accepted the invitation.

I had just completed a long, difficult summer traveling and working, but I knew I had to prepare myself for this trip. I approached a longtime friend to help out. Chris, who graduated a year or two ahead of me in high school, had reconnected with me at church ten years earlier. Today he is a football coach and knowledgeable enough to help me with my physical training. He decided to accept the challenge and requested a meeting to hammer out a possible game plan. We decided to meet every Tuesday and Thursday at my house to work out. These sessions started slowly as Chris watched and learned my capabilities. We purchased the equipment we needed, and the workouts accelerated. Part of Chris's strategy was mentioning upcoming exercises to prepare my mind for the challenge, which is why he kept saying: "Wait until you roll up the hill!"

Well, finally the day came to understand this roll-up-the-hill thing. It was a cold, dry day, and we had just finished the last typical exercise in our workout. Chris asked me to pick a hill. I chose sheepishly, not certain what was next. He then instructed me to roll down the hill I had chosen. It seemed simple enough—almost fun. Then once I was at the bottom, he instructed me to roll back up the hill. The particular hill I had chosen was the one in front of my house. My wife and I had put a lot of money into getting grass to grow on that hill, so it was a soft hill for the roll down. The real problem had just surfaced: that hill was very steep! Yet Chris encouraged me to roll back up the hill. Needless to say, I did, and my new workout suit was covered with everything that was previously on the hill. (Later that day, Lynn saw my workout clothes, and she thought we had completely lost our minds. Maybe we had.)

While enduring this workout regimen, I met another man with a similar story. I was speaking at a conference in Tennessee, and I met the keynote speaker. He had suffered a traumatic brain injury from a gunshot wound to the head during a convenience-store robbery. As he was recovering, he met a football coach, and this coach took him to a hill as well. As he was relearning to walk, the coach called over two of his college-level players and told them to drag the man down the hill. Once they had done that, he had them drag this man back up the same hill. Weeks went by, and every day this man was dragged, working all he could on his own, down and back up that same hill. After a few weeks, the coach had the players walk beside him down the hill and then help him back up. After six weeks, he was walking up and down the hill on his own. The night I met him, he walked onto the stage to deliver his keynote address. As he told his story, I sat in the back of the room and could not contain my smile. I thought of Chris and couldn't wait to tell him that our hill was not the only one.

Over the months that followed the start of our workouts, Chris found other interesting ways to get me back into shape. My initial reaction to these ideas of his was rarely positive. I would think to myself, "You must be crazy! Don't you remember that I have cerebral palsy?" However, I never voiced these concerns out loud. Chris was well aware of my abilities, so any complaining on my part just led to a longer, more difficult workout. He simply followed the same pattern with each new exercise. He started the hill exercise by running alongside me while I rolled, stopping me at the right spot. Then, as I gained more control, he would only help me stop if I needed the help. This past week, he didn't even go down the hill with me at all. He suggested that I exercise control. So I rolled the hill alone, and we both celebrated another victory. About 99 percent of the time, Chris was right, and my workouts follow this pattern:

I struggle.

I endure.

I hurt.

I ultimately accomplish the goal he set before me.

The hill is still special. The first day we rolled up the hill, I spent a lot of time thinking about that exercise. I was overwhelmed with memories of another hill. When I was young, my friends and I would play on the hill in front of my parents' house. We would wrestle and end up rolling down the hill. We would play war and pretend to be shot and roll down the hill. Sometimes we would just roll down the hill to roll down the hill! Never mind the gravel road at the bottom. Never mind the scrapes and bruises from not stopping soon enough to avoid said gravel road. We were just having fun.

That's what struck me.

What I used to do for fun I now do for function.

But it's still fun.

The work of rolling up that hill allows me to find joy in things I could not otherwise do. As my strength and agility improve, the list of things I cannot accomplish diminishes. Things like traveling to the Philippines. On that trip, I was asked to walk more than I have had to walk at any point I can remember. Walking along alleyways, upstairs, over rugged spots in a path, up a beach—you name it; I walked it. In short sections, perhaps, but I walked it nonetheless. Just seven months ago, that would not have been possible, but now I am capable of so much more.

Unlike many of the stories in this book, this one is still active. Chris and I still have our workouts every Tuesday and Thursday. We continue to work on my strength and agility. While I don't know what might be next in my journey, I do know that I'm doing the work of being prepared. I'll be mobile enough for whatever opportunities come my way. With my determination and Chris's help, I can get even stronger and even more mobile.

You see, in life, our greatest challenges often open the door to our greatest joys. Those workouts opened the door to going on that mission trip to the Philippines. Those workouts give me the confidence to try other new experiences.

They are not easy.

They often are not fun.

They often are not how I want to spend a morning.

But they are liberating.

So I keep it up. Not because I find great joy in the workouts but because I find great joy in the freedom and confidence the workouts give me. That's what so many people don't seem to understand. While we are living in the glory days of the past, when everything was easy because we were young and strong, I am getting ready for the glory days of the future, when doors will unexpectedly open and yield joy I didn't even know exists.

I am preparing today for a greater tomorrow.

I am working today for a stronger tomorrow.

I am struggling today to be free tomorrow.

So do you think you've had some good days up to this point?

Wait until you roll up the hill.

10

SPEAK PERSISTENCE

"Of course you are going to make it. What other choice do you have?"
—*Brenda Goodman, Mike's mom*

Faith expresses itself best in endurance.

It was just one of those days. You know the kind I am talking about. Those days when everything just seems to be falling apart on you, and you're just not sure it's all worth it anymore. I was honestly not sure whether to just gut it out or drop to the floor and throw a temper tantrum like a two-year-old. At the moment, the temper tantrum was my favorite idea. Things just weren't going as I would have liked, and I wasn't certain what to do next. I thought, and tried, and worked, and considered, and prayed, and...nothing.

So I did what any fussy two-year-old would do: I called my mom. I began telling her about all my disappointments and how tough life really was. I suppose I was hoping to get a bit of sympathy from her, but I got...nothing. I tried making the story more fatalistic and threw in a little more drama and waited...still nothing. Finally I just gave up and said, "Well, I'll make it through." Her response was not what I expected and definitely not what I wanted to hear. Without missing a beat, she answered, "Of course you're going to make it. What other choice do you have?" I was stunned. Where was the compassion? Where was the sympathy? Where was the "poor baby" I was looking for?

After I got over my disappointment, I thought about her response for quite a while. I just couldn't get it out of my mind. Perhaps because it wasn't what I expected to hear and perhaps because I knew it was true. In the end, I was going to make it. I was going to make it because, in the end, I was not going to give up. Mom knew that, and so did I. So "poor baby" was not the right answer, even if it was what I wanted to hear. Mom gave me the right answer.

Now, this was not the first time I had experienced this lesson. Like most profound statements, this was profound because it rang true with past experiences. I worked at a pizza place when I was a teen. I would spend what seemed like endless hours making pizzas for everyone who came through the door. Each night, and especially after football games, there would be a few moments that seemed almost impossible. In those moments, the pizza orders would start to pile up, and at times, there were more orders than there were tables in the restaurant. Sometimes I even felt that there were more orders than there were people in our small southern town.

And I would want to panic.

As those orders would pile up, I would think that behind each piece of paper was a hungry human who was going to be furious with me if they did not get their dinner, and soon. Even though the restaurant was not considered a fast-food joint, those people wanted their food fast. So I wanted to panic.

I learned something in those moments.

If I panic, nobody eats.

If I keep looking at that growing pile of tickets, I will panic.

The more I looked at that pile, the worse I felt.

The more hopeless the situation seemed.

The less I believed that I would ever get home.

So right there in that pizza kitchen, I devised a plan that I still use to this day. I refused to look at the pile. I would just focus on the ticket in front of me. Make that one pizza, and then pick up another ticket and focus on the next, and so on.

You get the strategy, right?

As long as I kept focusing on one ticket at a time and did not stop making pizza, everyone ate. Almost everyone left the restaurant happy.

One pizza at a time, I dealt with a tsunami of human hunger. The strategy was brilliant. (Or at least I thought so.)

It got me through many crowded nights in the pizza place.

It kept me employed.

It kept people fed.

All of those were important to me.

So I just kept making one pizza at a time.

Now, you might be thinking that what you want is a stress-free life. You might actually hope and pray for a life free from piled-up orders that seem impossible to fill. But that is really not what you want. One of the other employees, who was tired and frustrated at the moment, said to me, "I wish people would stop ordering pizza!" I replied, "No, you don't." He responded with, "Well, I wish these tickets would stop piling up!" I said again, "No, you don't." He looked at me with a level of frustration that communicated something between, "I don't understand," and, "I think I'm going to kill you," so I explained. "If there are no piles of tickets, there are no paychecks." He then changed his tune and said, "Oh yeah." So we kept making pizzas.

Life is just like that. While you may think that you want a stress-free life, the truth is that virtually everything that gives life meaning adds stress. However, those same things give life value. Those same things give life joy. To live without experiencing the difficulties of life is to live without experiencing the joys of life.

Relationships are stressful…and they add meaning.

Marriage is stressful…and it adds love.

Kids are stressful…and they add joy.

Vacation is stressful…and it adds fun.

Life is stressful…and it is well worth living.

The truth is that our problem is not that we have stress. Our problem is that the stress in our lives makes us want to stop trying. We begin to think that we are just too tired, too broken, too hurt, too lonely, too weak, too stupid, and too far-gone to make it through.

This is a lie.

We are never too far-gone.

Now, don't get me wrong. We really are tired, broken, hurt, lonely, weak, and stupid. There is no sense in denying the reality of our situation, but we are never too far-gone. The difference between someone who loses and someone who overcomes is really simple: those who overcome are those who don't quit. They trust that they will make it through and accept that they have no other choice, and so they just endure. They endure until they are free. They still may be tired, broken, hurt, lonely, weak, and stupid. But they are free. Free because they have found that stress can't take them out. Free because they have learned that no amount of struggle can stop them. Free because they have endured through the pain, brokenness, loneliness, and stupidity. They have endured it all, and now they are free.

You see, many people allow situations to drive them. Survivors don't do that at all; survivors drive situations, and not because they are smart, or strong, or heroic. They drive situations because they are determined. They refuse to quit. They refuse to give up. They simply refuse to lose. Instead, they choose to be free.

Now, you may be thinking that this is just some self-awareness nonsense that is going to leave you empty at the end of the day. The truth is that victory goes to the survivor every time. We don't like that truth because it doesn't always seem fair. The survivor may not be the strongest, the best, or the most heroic. In fact, the survivor may not even be the one who *should* win. Simply put, the survivors are the ones who don't quit. By not quitting, they win. By not quitting, they find freedom. By not quitting, they overcome. Victory, my friend, goes to the survivor.

This brings me back to the conversation with my mom. She taught me not to give up. Though what she said may have seemed a little harsh to you, she was right. She said exactly what I needed to hear at that moment. If she had played into my self-pity, she may have strengthened some deep-seated belief that the situation was hopeless. By being caring, she could have confirmed hopelessness, and that would have placed my future in danger. Instead, she saw hope and spoke about that hope in definite terms. She knew I would make it. She knew I would never quit. She convinced me that what she knew was real. So I pressed on and didn't quit. I survived.

In that moment, I relearned something from my teenage years. If there are no tickets, there are no paychecks.

There is more to that truth.

While a normal flow of tickets produces a normal level of pay, extra tickets could lead to extra pay. If there are an extraordinary number of tickets, then there are more people ordering pizzas, and all those tickets may mean a bonus is on its way. Higher levels of business lead to higher levels of business income, which lead to higher levels of employee pay. So if I face great levels of stress and don't quit, then there will be a great payoff for my endurance. It simply makes sense. Panic, and nobody eats. Keep your head, and there's a payoff. Endure greatly, and the payoff may be greatness.

So we come to one of my favorite questions: what are you going to do?

If you give up, you lose.

If you keep on, it hurts.

If you stay steady, it pays off.

If you never quit, you're free.

If you endure greatly, you find greatness.

Not so sure you can make it? Of course you can. What other choice do you have?

11

SPEAK PERSPECTIVE

"Fight for this, please."

—*Tina Hilson, Mike's wife*

My resolve directly impacts the dreams of others.

Some years ago, I faced a dramatic reversal in my personal and professional life. It was one of those moments that could have simply put an end to a person's hopes, dreams, and future. To be honest, that was kind of what I thought was happening. I really believed, at that moment, that my career was over. I was ready to give in. I began to think of what I might do next. Honestly, a degree in Christian ministries and a resume that is almost entirely lived out as a pastor doesn't exactly qualify a man for a wide range of career choices. So, although my list of choices was fairly short, I was making it. I began asking myself how I could facilitate my departure with the least amount of collateral damage to the church I was leading. What could I tell people? What could I not tell people? How much of this could be painless for everyone but me? I hate to admit it, but I had given up.

Now, no one else knew I had given up. I didn't tell anyone that I was done. I was just going to keep it to myself until the time was right. However, my wife knew. After years of dating and marriage, she could read me like a book. She knew what I was thinking, and she knew that there wasn't a lot of time left. As we sat one night and discussed how bad

I thought my life was and how few options I felt I had, she looked at me with pleading eyes and said, "Mike, fight for this. Please!"

At that moment, I woke up. Somehow, in my own self-pity, I had forgotten that this was more than just my life. Tina and I have been together since we were sixteen years old. She has been part of every decision I have ever made. We have grown up together, endured together, fought together, lost together, and won together. We had already accomplished more in our lives than either of us thought possible, and now, somehow, I selfishly had decided to give up without talking to her about it first. My decision to surrender was about to cost her...and I had not considered that.

To fully understand our situation, you need a little more background. When we were first married, I had insisted that she develop a career path of her own. She resisted. I begged her to find something she could do apart from my career. I wanted to know that she would be all right if anything happened to me. I thought I was acting in her best interest, and many would agree. In reality, it was, again, selfishness. I did not want to carry the burden alone. I did not want to be solely responsible for her and our kids. I wanted her to help me carry the load. She finally explained it to me in a way that I could understand. I had always been driven. I had dreams and goals that I was determined to reach. I didn't understand anyone not having those, but she finally explained to me that her ambition in life was to walk beside me as I pursued my ambition. Her ambitions were all wrapped up in me.

Talk about pressure!

Knowing that, I had selfishly made a rash decision about those ambitions without even consulting her. My resolve was having a direct impact on her dreams, and I didn't even realize it. So, with pleading eyes, she asked me to fight for this.

So I did.

Partly because she asked.

Mostly because she was right.

I just couldn't give up. Her dreams and plans were wrapped up in what we were doing. This was not just some job I had landed; it was our purpose for being. Not to mention, we had the kids to think about. Their whole world was tied up in this thing that I did as a job. They didn't know anything else. Sure, I could move to another place and be fine, but that would have been selfish. They would have suffered—taking them from what they know, friends they had made, a church family they had grown to love, their school, and a community they called home. My escape would have caused great harm to those I loved most. I simply needed to think more clearly.

Giving up is often incredibly selfish. To quit just because it is too hard for me is to ignore the needs and dreams of those who have sacrificed with me to help. Even if I think I can't go on for myself, I must go on for them. I must realize that I am not the only one with a stake in this. I must further realize that my family is not the only family with a stake in this. There are other families, other individuals, and other people who have sacrificed with us to see our dreams become a reality. To quit is to let them down as well. In fact, my desire to quit so that I might find some short-lived sense of peace could affect the lives of literally hundreds of other people. I should really think about them, shouldn't I?

Well, maybe you're thinking to yourself that my situation is not like yours. Sure, when a pastor quits, a lot of people get hurt, but maybe you think that it's just you in your situation.

Not true.

No one is that isolated. There are always others who care about you and what you are doing, and they will always be affected by what you choose to do and not do. Your selfish quitting will hurt them. Unless you have moved yourself into some cabin in the backwoods of Montana miles away from anyone and stayed there for, oh, say forty years, you are not isolated. Your decisions affect others.

Think about them.

Just for a moment.

Forget your own fear.

Set aside your own failure.

Lay down your own pain.

And notice them.

You might be thinking: "What about me? Don't I matter? Don't my feelings and desires count? Don't I get a break sometimes?" The answer is yes, but the reality is that quitting is going to hurt you as well. You just haven't realized it yet. Often we run away from something difficult before we take the time to consider what the real effect on our own life is going to be.

Once I start quitting, when do I stop?

Once I allow failure to overtake me, where does that lead?

Once I give in to despair, when does that end?

Honestly, quitting almost never solves the problem.

Certainly there are times for transition in life. Those times need to be considered by everyone who could be affected by the decision. As long as the transition is more than just quitting and running away, then certainly there are times when changing course is the right thing to do. All too often we haven't considered everything. All too often we have only considered our own feelings and not those of others. All too often our own pain causes poor choices, which in turn cause more pain.

The answer to this dilemma is counsel. The counsel of others who have a stake in our decision will help us to make better choices. When I was deciding based on my own feelings and not considering those of others, I was well on the way to a disastrous choice. When I brought into the equation the thoughts of someone who knew me, loved me, believed in me, and was fighting with me, the decision-making process took a new direction. Tina helped me to see a new reality. She helped me to see a better day. She helped me to see another way.

Big choices require good counsel.

Good counsel comes from well-informed people.

Well-informed people love me enough to help me fight on.

So you want to quit? Are you tired of the fight? Bruised by the struggle? Ready to run?

Wait.

Talk.

Listen.

Consider them, not just you.

Then decide.

And just maybe, through pleading eyes, you will hear: "Fight for this…Please!"

By the way, since I stayed, life has never been better.

12

SPEAK TRUST

"I trust you."

—*Lynn Watson, Robert's wife*

Past failure is no guarantee of future results.

In 1999, I began what I expected to be the longest drive of my life. It was early evening, and Lynn and I had just begun our fifty-mile commute home. In Washington, DC, this trip can take anywhere from one and a half to three hours. We had been married for a little more than seven years, and I was deeply involved in my hobby of being a day trader in the stock market. Lynn did not really like this choice of hobbies for me. She is not very keen on risk, and day trading can be very volatile. I knew that all too well on this afternoon. That was why I expected it to be the longest drive of my life.

You see, on this day, I needed to break the news to Lynn that I had been on a losing streak. After a single week of losing money, I had dug us into a hole that I knew would take years for us to dig ourselves out of. Somehow, on this drive, I had to tell her how much I had lost, and the amount contained a significant number of zeros. I fully expected a complete meltdown. I was bracing myself for the worst. Almost hyperventilating, shaking, and sweating, I felt sick. Finally, after fighting it as long as I could, I just blurted it out: "Lynn, I lost 60 percent of everything we have this week." Then I sat and waited.

In that eternity of silence between delivering the bad news and hearing the reaction, I wondered how long she would be mad at me. Would she ever trust me again? Would she insist that I stop investing all together? What would she say? She couldn't possibly make me feel any worse than I already did, so I supposed anything she said would have been fine at that moment. Anyway, I was ready for whatever came my way.

I deserved it.

I had earned it.

I heard her taking a breath…and I knew it was coming…

"I trust you," she said.

What? No screaming? No crying? No panic? No anger? Nothing I had expected?

"No, really," I repeated. "I lost 60 percent of everything this week." I just assumed she hadn't heard me or perhaps hadn't understood. I needed her to know what had happened. I had to get this right, and I was ready for her reaction, whatever it may be.

"I heard you," she said, "and I trust you."

Now it really was quiet.

We rode for a while in silence as I processed the guilt of having lost so much of our future and contrasted that with the comfort of knowing that my wife trusted me anyway. I knew that much of what I had lost was entirely my fault. I could not even blame a bad market, really. Even though there was a downturn, the truth was that I hadn't been doing my job very well, and in losing track of the market's movement, I lost all the money. I was to blame, and she still trusted me.

What was I supposed to do with that?

Isn't it funny how, as humans, we can struggle just as much with someone's trust and acceptance as we do with their anger and rejection? Sometimes we almost want our loved ones to be angry with us to somehow give us a little relief from our own guilt. Yet that isn't always what happens. Sometimes they just choose to trust us, and then we must work through what to do next. What does it mean to be trusted by someone when you have almost lost faith in yourself? How should you react, and what should your next step be? Who was right? Was Lynn's trust valid, or was my sense of failure valid? Or both?

In my case, Lynn's trust allowed me to step back into the market, change my approach, and regain much of what we had lost. Her trust told me that I could succeed. Even in the face of failure, her trust convinced me of an old market adage in reverse.

Past failure is no guarantee of future results.

When someone has a level of faith in us that supersedes our own failure, it gives us the strength we need to move on. Honestly, success and failure are not really measured in short-term results. While a winning day feels good and gives us cause for momentary celebration, it cannot make us any more than a single losing day can break us. We do not win or lose in the short term. We win or lose in the long term. One week of failure on the stock market did not need to deeply affect me. It was, after all, just one week. Lynn saw that. I didn't. She understood that I was more than capable of gaining back all that I had lost—and perhaps even more. She trusted that, in the end, I would do the right thing and all would be fine. That trust allowed me to move on.

When those who mean the most to us trust us, it gives us a great sense of security. Honestly, as human beings, success or failure in our business or work falls a distant second in importance to our success or failure in relationships. Any healthy person knows that the most important thing in life is our relationships. So if the ones closest to you are still with you, still love you, and still trust you, everything else is secondary.

I should pause here to say a word to those who have already focused so much on work and success that the relationships are gone. Don't lose hope…just change your course. You must finally come to grips with the fact that success at work is not your greatest goal. You need to deal with the reality that you could gain all the wealth in the world and still be the poorest of all if you fail to maintain healthy relationships in your life. Your money and success may bring you financial security, but only loving relationships will bring you emotional security. If you must choose between the two, always choose relationships. If all this seems like it can't possibly be true, please trust me, and give it a try. It will make sense in the end.

When everything else is secondary to relationships and relationships are strong, we truly become secure in our lives. This security gives us permission to take risks. If the work and wealth are secondary and the relationships that are most important are secure, we can take the risk necessary to find success. That's right; secure relationships increase the probability of success. A stable, relational world allows me to make clear and rational decisions about risk.

When my self-worth is tied to my net worth, I am weak. I will then have a codependent relationship with my work life. I cannot really control it or risk it because I cannot live without it. Make no mistake, it can exist without me. Allowing work and wealth to be a measure of my own self-worth creates a recipe for failure.

There is an old rock song that fits here. The band 38 Special made the song a hit in the 1980s. It's called "Hold on Loosely." The chorus teaches a profound truth:

"Hold on loosely, but don't let go.

If you cling too tightly, you're gonna lose control."

I cannot hold on loosely to something I believe I must have. The more I'm convinced that I can't exist without it, the tighter I hold on to it. The tighter I hold on, the more likely I am to choke the very life out of it. And once it is dead, it is dead, and I am lost. This risk is intensely great with things like money, fame, or success, but with people, the issue is different. With relationships, there is a very real two-way street. While I may have a need for my wife or children, I don't have to hold on with a choking grip. Why? Because they are just as interested in staying with me as I am in staying with them. Money, fame, and success are always running away. They come and go so quickly and easily. Once I gain some more money, I also gain an innumerable amount of new ways to lose that money. In time, I exist only to replenish the money that keeps pouring out of my hands. Fame and success are much the same. With relationships, I find that those I love are running toward me and not from me. So, while things and possessions are coming only to go, people are coming to stay.

That gives me security.

Security in something more.

Security in something that will stay.

Security in someone who will pursue me as intently as I pursue him or her.

Security that is not codependent but interdependent.

Security that is, well, secure.

That sense of security gives me courage. Now that I know that the thing I need most is chasing me as hard as I am chasing it (the relationship), I can make bold decisions. Since Lynn trusted me in the worst of moments, I came to realize that her love and trust were not on the line when I made an investment. Even if I lost it all, she was still going to be there. So I could have courage. Tomorrow was not going to be the end; it would be a new day. I could lose all the money we had and still have what was most important: Lynn.

Now, let me be careful here. I am not talking about a haphazard courage or a foolish courage. Foolishness should never be confused for courage. It is only foolishness. It was time for me to do my research, test my theories, apply all the knowledge I had and all the insight I could find, and then have courage to move on with a plan. To be honest, I stopped looking for the short-term gain of day trading altogether and moved to a long-term approach to investing. This was not a change based on fear but one based on faith. Her faith gave me courage.

I could go out and conquer because the fair maiden back at the castle was anxiously awaiting my return and fully expecting to hear the heroic stories of my epic victories.

OK, that was a little over the top, but you get the point, right? Her faith in me gave me courage to face challenges and overcome obstacles. She made me strong. She believed in me, and so I believed in me. It wasn't very complex. I was not going to fail her. Not without the fight of my life.

This brings us to determination. Knowing that others believe in me, have faith in me, and are depending on me gives me great determination. As long as it's within my power to overcome, I will.

I will not quit trying, because they do not quit expecting.

I will not quit fighting, because they do not quit loving.

I will not quit believing, because they do not quit believing in me.

Shortly after Mike married his wife, Tina, he had an interesting conversation with her dad. During the conversation, Tina's dad told Mike, "I have never worried about you and Tina. You have always made it clear that you would work as many jobs in whatever circumstances were necessary in order to take care of her. I believe that to be true about you. So I don't have to worry about my daughter." That level of trust goes in both directions. Tina, too, is willing to work in any way to bring success to their marriage and family. That kind of determination is key to a great marriage. It's the same determination that exists between Lynn and me. It is a determination that just will not accept failure as an option.

13

SPEAK LOVE

"When you get up there to that church, you just love and take care of those people, and they will love and take care of you."

—*Robert Freeman, Mike's grandfather*

Love is the key to true leadership.

In 1992, I accepted the position of senior pastor at Sandy Ridge Wesleyan Church in Hickory, North Carolina. Up until this time, I had worked on staff with another pastor taking the lead role. Now for the first time, I was going to be the leader. Both of my grandfathers had served as pastors in the Wesleyan Church, and so I felt the need to speak with each of them about my new assignment. So one spring afternoon, I took the journey over to Grandpa and Grandma Freeman's house, and I sat down in their living room to deliver the good news.

Now, you should know that my grandpa Freeman had a profound spiritual life. I had, on many occasions, watched as he initiated a time of prayer or testimony that ended up with everyone around in tears and in awe of the connection my grandpa had with God. So I was especially excited to hear what he had to say and have him pray for us. Of course, he did not disappoint. As Tina and I sat there listening to his advice, he paused and said, "Michael, when you get up there to that church, you just love and take care of those people, and they will love and take care of you."

Since that day, many powerful things have occurred in our pastoral work. Many opportunities for leadership and learning have come our way. We have had the opportunity to meet and learn from some of the most gifted leadership educators in the country. This insight from my aging grandfather is still the best leadership advice I have ever received.

You see, the ability to truly lead someone is born from and earned through the capability to truly love someone. Now, I am not talking about loving someone like I love my wife, my children, my parents, or my grandparents. I am talking about loving the people we lead with an appropriate love that drives us to give them our very best—not out of obligation but out of compassion. Not to earn a paycheck but to earn a relationship. True leadership requires love. True leadership is born from love.

Sometimes young pastors will ask me whether they should take a job at a particular church or in a particular ministry. My answer is always the same. I want to know that they have done their research, are qualified for the position, and whether or not they have the initial support of the church leadership core. After all of that is answered, we get to the most important matter: "Can you fall absolutely in love with those folks to the point that you would invest your life to make them better?" If the answer is yes, then I recommend they go. If the answer is no, then I recommend they keep looking. As overly simplistic and old-fashioned as it sounds, they just cannot effectively lead someone they cannot earnestly love.

In the end, the reason for this is quite simple. The only difference between leadership and manipulation is motive. When someone looks at a group of people, in any setting (church, politics, business, government, family, etc.), and sees them only as resources that can be exploited or used for that person's own gain, then that person is a manipulator. When someone looks at a group of people, in any setting (church, politics, business, government, family, etc.), and sees friends and companions who simply need a fresh outlook of the world or a new direction to travel in, then that person is a leader. The manipulator is in it for his or her gain. The leader is in it for the improvement of the people. What sets these two apart is a real, genuine, deep-seated love for those we lead.

The difficult part of this to grasp is that both manipulator and leader may make the same decisions. They may have the same external goals for the group or the organization. They may both lead in such a way that they are seen as successful. Likewise, they may both fail. When the manipulator succeeds, he or she is the one richly rewarded while others are left feeling used and exploited. When the leader succeeds, he or she too may be richly rewarded, but others will feel blessed to have been part of something that makes their lives and their world better.

A leader steers people to a place that makes them better.

A manipulator leads people to a place that makes him or her better.

And the difference between the two is love.

And so it is with everything we have written about in this book. We have told you story after story. We have given accounts of how things happened and how certain words, moments, insights, and advice spoke life into our lives. The one thing that holds true in every case is that the words came from a heart of love. Each person we have written about loves us. Each loves us differently, but each loves.

Love is what inspired the words that spoke life.

Love is what enveloped the delivery of those words.

Love is what made even the most difficult of those words acceptable to our ears.

It is really amazing what truth you can speak into the life of someone who knows your words are born from a place of love. You can say almost anything if the person you are speaking to knows that you love them and only want the best for them. Almost anything you say can bring life to that person. Words born out of love virtually always bring life.

Unfortunately, words born out of love have become all too uncommon in our world. It is far more common to hear words of anger, sarcasm, bitterness, and revenge. Somehow, in our culture, we have taken to using insulting words to describe people we actually love. It's almost as if we have forgotten how to use kind, loving language and instead have given in to the much cooler, hipper, hurtful language of our day.

This needs to stop.

We have not forgotten how to love.

We have forgotten how to communicate love.

We have forgotten how to lovingly communicate.

We have forgotten to start from a point of love for another person and let our words proceed from there.

So may we end this book with a challenge?

When you are speaking to your spouse, your kids, your siblings, your parents, your coworkers, your employees, your church, your civic group, your supporters, your detractors, your friends, and, yes, even your enemies, speak lovingly…and, therefore, speak life.

You can actually start where this book ends. When you encounter people, love and take care of those people, and they will love and take care of you.

And then the world—at least the world around you—will be a much better place.

ABOUT THE AUTHORS

Robert Watson holds a bachelor's degree in social work from Salisbury University in Salisbury, Maryland, and a master's degree in nonprofit administration from the University of Maryland in Baltimore. He is the executive director of DateAble Inc., a nonprofit dating service for people with and without disabilities. He is also president of Independence Now, an independent-living center in Maryland and advises many other disability-advocacy organizations. Robert is married to Lynn, whom he met through DateAble. Robert has delivered many presentations all over the United States, Canada, Cuba, Australia, and the Philippines on a variety of topics, including disability awareness, advocacy, sexual-intimacy issues, and dating with a personal-care attendant present.

Pastor Mike Hilson is the senior pastor of the New Life Wesleyan Church in La Plata, Maryland. As senior pastor at New Life Wesleyan Church, he has led the congregation to significant growth. Since 1999, this single congregation of just less than one hundred attendees has multiplied into multiple churches and venues with over four thousand in regular attendance. He has also led the congregation into significant involvement in local and international relief work. Along with his work at New Life Wesleyan Church, he currently serves as the assistant district superintendent of the Chesapeake District of the Wesleyan Church and as a trustee to Southern Wesleyan University. He lives in La Plata with his wife, Tina.